PAINTBALL
STRATEGIES
AND TACTICS

BEGINNER TO ADVANCED

Leslie J. Cuneo

ISBN: 150083890X

ISBN 13: 9781500838904

DEDICATION

To my Son Michael John, for keeping me young
and giving me grey hair all at the same time.

Remember these three things:
Conditioning
Shoot and Move
Practice, Practice, Practice

DISCLAIMERS

Although the author and publisher have made every effort to ensure that the information in this book was correct at press time, the author and publisher do not assume and hereby disclaim any liability to any party for any loss, damage, or disruption caused by errors or omissions, whether such errors or omissions result from negligence, accident, or any other cause.

The information in this book is meant to supplement, not replace, proper Paintball training. Like any sport involving speed, equipment, balance and environmental factors, Paintball poses some inherent risk. The author and publisher advise readers to take full responsibility for their safety and know their limits. Before practicing the skills described in this book, be sure that your equipment is well maintained, and do not take risks beyond your level of experience, aptitude, training, and comfort level.

Blackburn Publishing
A division of
Blackburn Capital Group LLC
38 Blackburn Lane
Manhasset NY 11030

TABLE OF CONTENTS

PAINTBALL STRATEGIES

AND TACTICS

Paintball is a sport that was first played in 1981 in New Hampshire, in the United States. Since the game was initially played, it has grown much in popularity. The game has grown so popular that people even make a living from playing paintball. While you may not have the desire to compete at the highest of levels in order to earn money through paintball, there is nothing wrong with learning how to properly play the sport.

The game is played throughout the United States in various settings. You will find paintball arenas outdoors in the forest, in the desert, or inside various complexes. Paintball does not come without its fair share obstacles and steep learning curve to become a good player, which is why it is recommended to learn how to play the sport correctly so that you know what it takes to progress as a player.

When you spend time playing any type of sport, you want to maximize your experience throughout the entire process. From learning how to properly approach the game of paintball as a beginner to finding your place as a veteran, this book will teach you how to properly learn the game of paintball.

Playing paintball is naturally fun no matter your skill level. You can pick up casual games with friends and have a great deal of fun. The more you play, the greater desire you may have to become better. That is where this book can help. Throughout the book you can learn the basics of how to play the game, the types of weapons used, basic strategies to apply to win, and much more about how to progress positively in the game of paintball. Read this book to learn the ins and outs of paintball so that you can see just how fun it is to become one of the best in the sport.

2

A BEGINNER'S GUIDE TO GETTING STARTED IN PAINTBALL

First things first. Get down the fundamentals of paintball and understand how it is played on a basic level. If there is one characteristic all sports share with one another, it is players need to understand how to play sports at a fundamental level in order to be truly competitive. It is true that paintball is a sport that can be played solely for fun, but many people get a thrill out of paintball when they are competing at a high level with one another.

The Basics
Paintball is a sport that is either played by a team or individually. The goal of the game is to eliminate all of your opponents by hitting them with a paintball that you fire from your paintball gun (also known as paintball marker). Paintball is played in a series of rounds. Typical games of paintball are played where if a person is hit or tagged once by a paintball they are eliminated from the round. A round is over when all players on one side of the team are tagged by a paintball shot.

Every player is required to wear some type of protective gear on their body to prevent themselves from becoming severely injured. Padding is suggested for sensitive areas on your body such as your elbows, knees, crotch, neck, and your back. Masks to cover your face (and especially eyes) are usually required to be worn before you can begin playing the game. Each country and region has their own set of rules regarding paintballs, check the local rules to determine what you can and cannot do as you play.

Players who play paintball carry with them a paintball gun, a mask or goggle, and usually a pod or pod packs (where their ammunition is stored). Frequent players and those who compete in tournaments like to wear jerseys to represent their team or group of players who they frequently play with. Many players also wear gloves to help protect their fingers from harm. One of the most interesting aspects of paintball is that it has evolved to a level where some fields have ATVs or go-karts players can travel in to get to one side or the other.

Game Types

The most basic game type played in paintball is Elimination. In the Elimination game type players on both teams start on opposite sides of the playing field from one another and must find each other and eliminate all of their opponents. This is where the team aspect of the game comes into play. Players need to work together in order to win rounds and matches. It is wise to travel in small groups with one another to increase your chances of fending off opponents that you see in the battlefield.

Capture the Flag is another popular game type that many people who play paintball are familiar with. Capture the Flag works the same as Elimination, where you must shoot all of the other players on the opposing team to win, except that is not the only way to win. Each team has a flag in their base of operation that they must protect; in order to win in this game type a team must infiltrate the opposing side's territory to steal their flag and take it back to their base. Capture the Flag adds a whole new dynamic to the game where you have to worry about more than just yourself and your teammates, you have to make sure that the flag is secure in your base.

A game type of more advanced players is Ammunition Limits. In this game type you play either elimination, capture the flag, or another game type, except that you are limited on the amount of ammunition you can use in a particular round. You are required to reserve your ammo for when it matters most, making you second guess every shot you take.

Other popular game types include capturing hidden objects around the playfield, attacking a particular area with your team, or defending one location with your team for an allotted period of time. Games can last anywhere from several minutes to as long as hours. In some scenarios games can last up to days at a time, but those are reserved for the hardcore players.

Rules

A sport is not without its set of rules. Paintball has specific rules that all players must follow, no matter their location, the first being that practically no physical contact should occur between opposing players at any time. This means no hitting, shoving, or restraining another player as you play. All you can do is shoot opponents, and that's it.

Many arenas prohibit the act of overshooting, or shooting a player an excessive amount of times after they have been eliminated. Shooting an opponent too many times can result in minor injury. To play it safe, shoot an opponent a couple of times to make sure they are tagged and that's it, refrain from overshooting.

Ramping and wiping are two more common practices that are banned from most paintball fields. Ramping involves modifying your paintball gun to automatically shoot faster than your trigger finger. This is banned from most arenas, yet it is allowed to some extent in certain tournaments. Wiping is when a player wipes paint off their body to hide the fact that they've been hit. Wiping is regarded as a serious violation of rules and is punished severely in most places.

BASIC TACTICS

The game type, your positioning, timing, and understanding of your opponent and surroundings are all basics to winning in paintball. Remember, at the end of the day you are playing to win. Therefore, review the various tactics outlined in order to expand your understanding of how to approach the world of competitive paintball.

Flanking Maneuvers

In paintball, flanking is positioning yourself and your teammates so that you surround your opponents on at least two separate sides. Flanking is an important strategy to be knowledgeable about in order to win matches when playing paintball. Not only should you work with your teammates to flank your opponents to give you a winning edge, but you should do what it takes to prevent yourself and your teammates from being flanked.

First, let's get down what it takes to flank an opponent or group of opponents. You need at least one other person to get into a position that is advantageous for you to either pin down and prevent your opponent from advancing, or to shoot and hit them. Communicate with your teammate your desire to flank an opponent and then make a move together to surround the opposing team. If necessary, either provide cover fire for a teammate who is moving into a flanking position or shoot cover fire for yourself to intimidate the other team and prevent them from hitting you or your teammates as you get into position.

Secondly, what may be more important than learning how to flank is to know how to prevent yourself and your teammates from being flanked. Winning a game is all about having superior defense, it does not matter how good you are individually if you cannot help your team achieve victory. Talk to your teammates and let one another know where the opposing team is located on the field at all times. When you see a couple of opponents move into position to flank, do your best to prevent them from progressing.

Shoot in front of them to make sure they are aware that you have your sights on them. If they continue to proceed in flanking position, it would be wise to try and focus on defending one side in particular with your teammates. The worst scenario you can be in when playing paintball is being pinned down by the opposing team as they take you and your teammates out one by one. If necessary, tell your teammates to move further back on the field in order to prevent yourselves from being flanked by your opponent.

Strong Side Attack
Many players feel that it is necessary to even the playing field and to distribute amongst one another to cover as much ground as possible. One overlooked strategy in paintball matches is to occasionally make everyone on your team push to overtake one side of the playing field. This strategy is known as a strong side attack, and it is a proven tactic that can help your team have the winning edge in a match.

In a strong side attack all of the players on your team agree to advance to one side of the field. This can work to your favor when executed properly. As everyone pushes to one side of the map you should all be ready to cover all paths your opponents may come from, that way you are ready to take out any targets. By overwhelming your opponents on one side you can quickly flank them and eliminate about half of them in the opening minutes of a round.

A strong side attack is only effective when your team is working together and everyone is looking out for one another. Designate someone who is a fast mover and quick shooter to run point and lead the way to take out as many targets as possible. Have at least a couple of people behind him to provide cover fire, a few others in the middle, and at least one or two people to cover you all from behind. As you push to one side of the map you should make it your primary objective to eliminate more opponents than team members you lose. If this is accomplished, then you will give your team an instant advantage for the round.

Trial and Error

Work together with your teammates to practice various strategies out on the paintball field. Every person and group of players has different attributes that can help them work better in a particular setting. As an example, fast players may find the flanking maneuver more advantageous for them, while slower players may feel the strong side attack strategy would work in their favor better.

As you progress through the game of paintball, play with a variety of strategies and see which works best for you. Keep in mind that what may work on one set of opponents may not work on another. Adapt your strategies through trial and error by practicing them on various opponents so that they will be as effective as possible, no matter who you play against.

4

THE IMPORTANCE OF KNOWING
YOUR WEAPON

Your paintball gun is literally your heart and soul in the sport of paintball. This piece of equipment can make or break your experience, so make sure that you are playing with a gun that you feel confident with. There are a variety of guns available for use, including pistols that you can carry in case you run out of ammunition for your primary weapon.

Practice with a few different types of guns to see what you like the best. Some people prefer lighter guns that shoot faster but that have less accuracy; others like to use slower guns that have better accuracy so that they don't miss their target. The only way you're going to figure out what fits your specific play style is to try different paintball guns until you feel comfortable with a specific type. Once you find one that fits, stick to it and use it in all of your target practice and matches to help build your confidence and natural reflexes using that weapon.

No matter what you do, you must make sure that you are comfortable carrying your paintball marker for hours at a time. After playing paintball for several hours (and in some cases days), holding your marker can become extremely tiring. Do your best to build up your physical stamina as it will prove to be most beneficial in your development in the sport.

Paintball Marker Types

Two types of paintball guns are used by players: mechanical and elec-tropneumatic. Each has its own distinct features to take note of. To find the perfect match for you, study both types to see which you would feel more comfortable using.

Mechanical markers are seen as the more traditional types of paintball guns. These weapons have five ways they mechanically operate: pump or bolt action, double action, blowback semi-auto, blow forward semi-auto, and pneumatically operated semi-auto. Each affects the trigger and rate of fire in various ways to cater towards a specific playing style.

Pump or bold action paintball markers operate very similar to bolt action rifles or pump action shotguns. The mechanism of the marker on these weapons must be reset manually in between each shot. These are now seen as "old school" weapons. A pump or bold action paintball market can still come in handy since many pistols are in this form.

For a faster shooting weapon double action markers are available. With these guns the trigger mechanism fires and resets the firing mechanism, just like a double action revolver gun. Your rate of fire can increase by using these types of markers.

Semi-automatic weapons are highly favored in the sport of paint-ball because of their increased rate of fire. The blowback semi-auto, blow forward semi-auto, and pneumatically operated semi-auto are three different weapons that have grown in popularity amongst the community of paintball for this reason. Having a faster shot can make a big difference when multiple opponents are within your crosshairs.

Paintball Markers and Trigger Modes

Paintball markers include: the hopper-fed markers, pump and stock classic markers, magazine-fed markers, pistols, and human-powered weapons. There are literally dozens and dozens of types of weapons to choose from in each category, with an assortment of manufacturers creating these weapons. Visit a local paintball shop to learn in detail the specifications of each paintball marker and for which type of player they suit.

There are four trigger modes mainly used in paintball markers: pump action, semi-automatic, fully automatic, and ramping. The latter is primarily banned from paintball arenas. The trigger mode applied to a weapon affects its rate of fire and accuracy.

Most markers are preset, meaning their rate of fire cannot be altered. Ramping is a feature that is available in some markers that allows you to automatically change the gun from a semi-automatic to a fully automatic state. When a gun is modified in this sense, it is viewed as misleading and is looked down upon and banned from many paintball arenas or playing fields. The problem with ramping is that it is hard to detect if a gun is using this feature, making it unenforceable in some situations.

5

MANAGING YOUR PLAYING TIME

How often do you plan on playing paintball? If you are serious about the sport, invest time and money into it properly. Purchase a gun and equipment that is of good quality so that you do not have to constantly spend money on renting items.

Build your skills so that your aim and accuracy are at a good percentage. The more you know your own weapon, the greater chance you have at hitting all of your targets. If possible, shoot your gun at targets three to five times a week. All you have to do is shoot your targets for about 30 minutes to an hour and you will see immediate improvement in your natural aiming and targeting abilities.

Dedicate at least one to two times a week towards playing in actual paintball matches. Practicing can make perfect, and engaging in matches with all types of opponents can help give you an understanding of how to compete against and win in all types of situations. There is a certain level of skill that is acquired by logging in a lot of hours playing in real matches. Work your way towards becoming a veteran by putting in the hours and work necessary, just like any other professional athlete would.

As you progress through the sport of paintball, you will begin to notice that being in shape can prove to be beneficial. Consider establishing an exercise regimen that involves running and weightlifting to help your agility and endurance. Anyone who has played paintball for an extensive period of time knows that after a while of playing, fatigue starts to kick in, altering your ability to perform at your highest level.

Practice with Friends

After playing paintball for an extended period of time you should have made quite a number of acquaintances and friends. Practice with the same people as much as possible and form a team together with all those that are serious about competing. Share strategies and tips with one another to help everyone improve their skills. Teammates are the most valuable asset you have in playing matches and winning.

Schedule at least one time a week where everyone can meet to practice and discuss strategies to implement on the field. You can all meet before you actually play paintball, review the matches you played after a session, or schedule a time of day other than the one you play on to get on the same page. Once you start to form a team the whole world of paintball begins to change.

Forming a team is an exciting aspect of paintball. You can choose to compete for fun and even enter tournaments if you'd like. Just remember to not let paintball ruin your friendships. Manage a balance of playing paintball with your friends and spending time doing other activities to keep you all feeling comfortable with one another.

Spend Time on Other Activities

Paintball is a major aspect of your life when you decide to compete at a high level to win tournaments and prove yourself amongst the best. Just because you dedicate a lot of time to paintball does not mean you should neglect your friends, family, and other priorities outside the realm of paintball. Put time aside during the week and on weekends to attend family events, focus on school and/or work, hang out with friends outside of paintball (your paintball friends can tag along too), and to do other things not related to paintball.

Set your priorities straight to avoid regretting that you focused too much time and energy on paintball. Never miss school or work in order to play or practice paintball. The game is always going to be around, so it is not wise to jeopardize other areas of your life in an attempt to get better at the game. Unless paintball is your primary moneymaker and you are winning tournaments, you should put it second to other more important priorities in your life.

Getting away from the sport for a few days at a time can clear your head and give you a new and better perspective when you return, especially after a tough loss or rough day on the field. Block out some time to focus on other hobbies or goals you have when paintball becomes too overwhelming. You can return to the sport when you feel ready to compete again, it's always going to be around.

6

KNOWING YOUR OPPONENT INCREASES YOUR ABILITY TO ACHIEVE VICTORY

Who are you facing? A fundamental aspect to learn in any sport is to know your opponent. When it comes to paintball you should first analyze the age of your opponents. Younger players are usually much quicker and more aggressive because they can make a push without getting hit. Older players tend to take things a bit slower, but can be a big threat because they have good aim and usually apply difficult strategies to counter. Do not crack under pressure,

Study Match Footage

If you are playing in a tournament, there is nothing wrong with becoming familiar with your opponent before your matchup. Check their team name online to see if any videos of their previous matches are posted. You may get lucky and run into some videos of your opponents competing in a tournament or scrimmage against another paintball team. Study opponents in detail to know their strengths and weaknesses so that you may counter them.

Take footage of the games that you play. You can install a camera next to your facemask to help you record your matches, or have someone record the field from a distance. It is impossible to catch every single second of gameplay, but recording your matches can give you insight on how your team responds to your opponents.

Review match footage with your entire team and break down everything that went right and wrong throughout each match. You have to be willing to accept your faults in order to understand what they are and limit them from being visible to other teams. Dedicate the time necessary to making adjustments where you feel it necessary to make your team stronger as a whole.

Take note of the strategies being used by opponents you frequently play against as they attempt to execute them during matches. Knowing which strategies your opponents commonly use can help you properly plan defensive maneuvers to prevent them from beating your team. Winning paintball is all about anticipation and knowing what your opponent is going to do next, it helps you adapt and win.

Breaking Down Players

Break down the skill level of each individual player you are going to play against. Determine who should match up with them, which side of the map they prefer, their role on the team, and other characteristics about them that could help you learn how to beat them one on one in the battlefield.

Take a look at the type of equipment they use. The weapons your opponents are using can be a telltale sign of the kind of players you are going to face against in the battlefield. For example, if your opponents appear to be using light weapons that shoot fast and have armor that is not heavy, they are probably a team that likes to rush their opponents. Another sign that your opponents like to rush are their age (the younger the more likely they are to rush) and their personality.

Understanding Play Styles

Players and teams all follow a set of rules when playing paintball. This limits every team's ability to apply a variety of strategies on the battlefield. Use that to your advantage so that you know all of the strategies that will be applied against you. When you have a good amount of knowledge on all the possible strategies that can be used against you, there is essentially nothing that will come as a surprise to you during a match.

Reading this book from start to finish will give you a lot of knowledge about paintball that you can instantly apply to the sport. Use the knowledge you gain here and then continue to add to your knowledge of paintball to be able to adapt to any situation that comes your way. It takes years of exposure to the game of paintball to learn the ins and outs of what the sport entails.

7

HOW TO FORM A TEAM

Creating a paintball team is a fun experience that you are definitely going to want to engage in when you start taking the sport seriously. With a team you can compete in tournaments, make lasting friendships, grow as a player, and get the most out of paintball. There is no shame in trying to find teammates if you primarily play alone; it is part of the game. Just as you would join any group of friends, find a job, or become part of any organization, you need to network to find a team.

Whenever you play paintball do you run into the same people over and over again? If this is the case and you regularly attend paintball alone, get in touch with one of the other paintball players you cross paths with. Let them know you'd like to play together whenever they are free so that you can see what it's like to play with teammates regularly.

A resource you may want to look into to find teammates is the Internet. Browse reputable forums to see if other players in your area are looking for people to play paintball with. You can find forums by searching for them on a search engine. There should be people looking to play. Meet with them and start playing some paintball.

As you start to form paintball connections inquire to see which players you play with have a team. Consider one of two options, either trying to join a team with established players, or forming your own team with other players who do not have a team. Which option you choose is determined by the amount of time you have, and your level of dedication to paintball in relation to your teammates.

If you join a team, you can learn a lot about how a team works and operates. The players should have a lot of experience to share with you to help get you adjusted to what it is like to play with the same set of players regularly. The benefit of joining a team is that it is established and you can start playing matches against other teams. The downfall is that they may either be more or less committed to the sport than you are.

Creating a team on your own can prove more beneficial for a variety of reasons. The first is that you can add people to the team that you really want to work with, as opposed to joining one without any real idea about every player in detail. Establishing a team independently can give you credibility amongst the paintball community. Since you will be the one to lead your team, people will recognize that and respect you more for your efforts.

The downside to creating your own team is that the responsibility may become overwhelming for you. Make sure that you can dedicate the proper amount of time towards managing team meetings, practices, scheduling matchups, and doing everything necessary to keep everyone engaged in the sport. It takes a big chunk of time out of your week to lead a team, so make sure you are ready for the challenge ahead. Take the lead if you feel you are ready to start your own team. If not, then join one, just make sure you are dedicated to the sport once you make any commitment.

Building Team Chemistry

Playing with other teammates is more than everyone being good. You have to "click" with one another. All that means is that you should all be able to enjoy the company of one another and have the same drive and desire to win. Teams that play well with one another not only spend a great deal of time on the paintball battlefield, they also spend a great deal of time together off the field. What this does for them is it helps everyone understand how each other does things, making it easier for everyone to use their intuition to adopt new strategies when competing.

Dedicate at least one to two outings a week where everyone spends time with one another doing something else besides playing or talking about paintball. You can still talk about paintball here and there, and make references to the game if you wish, but try to do other activities such as going to the movies, attending social events, and anything else that catches your interest

As a team you should all be physically fit. If possible, work out together to help improve your endurance and physical capabilities. When you all work out together you can help keep each other motivated and in tiptop physical shape. Believe it or not, but a 30- to 60-minute workout three to four days a week can go a long way in helping you and your teammates ensure you are ready for any opposing teams that come your way.

Practice scrimmages between one another to help everyone gain a better idea of all of your individual strengths and weaknesses. Depending on the size of your team, you can pair up to face off in two versus two matches, three versus three matches, or something similar. Mix and match various combinations to see who meshes well together and you could figure out which combination of people on your team work well in particular situations.

8

LEARNING ADVANCED STRATEGIES

The basic strategies involved in the sport of paintball are something you never want to forget. As you progress through the game it is also important to gain an understanding of more advanced strategies. These are strategies you want to learn to apply on your own and to be aware of so you can see them coming from your opponent. Take note about these commonly used advanced strategies to broaden your knowledge of paintball.

Run and Gun
There is so much running and shooting (gunning) involved with paintball it is always necessary to practice your skills as a shooter while you're on the move. Go over various drills with your teammates about different scenarios where you must run and shoot. The more you practice your accuracy while you are being shot at, the better chance you have at being able to hit opponents in a real match when you are overwhelmed. Running and gunning is not something you want to apply to your strategies all the time; it's more rather a necessary skill to have to be able to avoid messy situations.

If you and your teammates feel confident enough during a match, you can try to run and gun a round or two. Catch your opponents by surprise by having every member of your team rush them. This strategy has a great amount of risk involved, and it is hard to implement, but if executed correctly it can grant you victory during a match.

Run and gun involves a great deal of physical capabilities. It's recommended to sprint often to get your body conditioned to running frequently. Keep in mind that this strategy can leave you tired and vulnerable. Only apply it when you feel it necessary.

Leapfrogging towards Victory

One of the most commonly used advanced strategies in paintball is called leapfrogging. The basic principle of this strategy is for one person to move from one area of the field to the next while one or two of their teammates are providing cover fire. Leapfrogging is usually used in conjunction with other strategies such as flanking. It takes a bit of practice, knowledge of the field, and good aim to be able to keep your opponents out and help your teammates advance through the field.

Leapfrogging is an important strategy to apply when playing game types such as Capture the Flag or any other objective game. By working your way towards the flag or another object with minimal loss of teammates, you can increase your chances of victory. Leapfrogging works best when you have good accuracy, that way you punish your opponents for making an attempt to hit your teammates. Make sure the best shooters are bringing up the rear and providing excellent cover fire or else you will find it difficult to practice leapfrogging efficiently.

Defensive Lockdown

Instead of rushing out to pick off your opponents one by one, sit back and wait for them to come to you. Establish a perimeter where you do not let one person get through your defense. A defensive lockdown strategy requires a great deal of patience, intimidation, and precision with your weapons. Allowing even one person to get through the barrier you have established can cause disaster for you and your teammates.

In order to set up a true defensive lockdown you and all of your teammates need to become familiar with the field you are playing on. Study the area ahead of time if you are playing on a field for the first time. Knowing all the angles of where your opponent is going to try and penetrate your defense is important to securing everyone in a safe place.

Strong Side Fake

Do you recall from the "Basic Tactics" chapter what a strong side attack is? It's when your team all pushes to one side of the map to overwhelm your opponent. This isn't the only way to trick the other team. A strong side fake applies the basic principle of a strong side, except it confuses your opponent and leaves them completely vulnerable.

A strong side fake attack is used to make your opponent believe you are going to rush one side of the map. Basically your team advances and makes a big push on one side while someone else scouts the other. You make your presence on one side well known for a brief moment and then retreat back to the other side of the map. The goal is to trick your opponent into thinking you are going to all overpower them on one side, but in truth you will overpower them on another.

The strong side fake is a very risky tactic; only the best and most advance teams should practice this strategy. It requires a great deal of stamina and superior communication skills to be able to coordinate this type of strategy. Practice trial runs with your team a few times to see how you as a whole are able to coordinate this type of attack together.

Sticking to your Guns

Strategies are not perfected overnight. As you create strategies with your teammates you are going to want to stick with them for an extended period of time. Alter a few details here and there as you progress, but refrain from dropping or drastically changing a strategy if it does not work right away. Sticking to your guns and following your strategy is the only way you're going to know what does and doesn't work.

In the heat of battle it can be extremely difficult to focus and to follow your strategy. Many teams find it difficult to work in unison when they first form; this is where team chemistry comes into play. The more time you each spend playing together or the game in general, the better understanding you are all going to have of how to play. Keep playing and stick to your strategies to see what type of results you can produce as a collective unit.

9

PLAYING TO WIN

The game of paintball when played at a highly competitive level is played to win. That means you have to get serious and log in some hours where you train your body and mind to learn ways to succeed. To play to win you have to have a certain mindset. The following are various methods to practice so that you are playing to win.

Reflect and Adapt

Thinking about how you performed in a particular match or moment in a match is part of the process of getting better. The best athletes in the world are always open to getting better as a player. Think about any moments that stick out in your mind and what you feel you could have done better to help prevent yourself from getting hit, or helping your team win a particular battle or situation. Figuring out how you can continue to get better is going to help you become one of the best players in paintball.

Did someone get past you as you were trying to defend a particular area? If so, you are going to need to improve both your accuracy and speed. Having a quick trigger to eliminate opponents who run fast is a crucial skill to have against high level opponents in paintball. Without quick reflexes you may not be able to stop a fast team from progressing around the map to threaten your team.

One aspect of paintball many new players and teams overlook is the types of strategies other teams practice. Think about how you lost your last match and what your opponents did to outsmart your team.

What strategies did they apply? Figuring out what exactly was the root cause of your loss can help you know how to counter that strategy and prevent you from losing to it in the future.

Speak with other more advanced teams about what they feel you as an individual can do to help your team. Also, be open to listen to constructive criticism about how your team as a whole can work together to produce more positive results. Part of growing as a player and a team is getting an outside view about what it is you are doing right and wrong and adapting your playing style so that you can generate the most success possible in every match.

Discipline is key to Success

How disciplined are you to sticking to your workout routine, collaborating with your teammates, listening to constructive criticism, and staying focused on becoming better at paintball in general? Check your status at the end of every week to gauge your overall progress. As long as you are putting in the time to try and get better, your skills and abilities will naturally grow in paintball.

Write a schedule for times throughout the week when you will dedicate yourself to practicing paintball in some way. Dedicate a few hours throughout the week to target practice, more to going over strategies for teammates, reading new tips and pointers about how to compete, updates on weapons that have yet to be released, and all relevant content related to paintball. As you begin to immerse yourself into the world of paintball, you will have so much knowledge of the sport you will become a veteran that people will seek advice from.

Did you know your diet could play a big factor on how focused and disciplined you can become. Eating healthier can help make your workouts easier to accomplish, and for you to get and remain in shape. Start eating foods more fruits and vegetables to give you the proper amount of energy and nutrition. Healthy meals can help provide your body with a good amount of energy to prevent fatigue in long matches, giving you the willpower to remain focused during the most intense of matches.

Keep your spirits up and think positively. Paintball is going to have its ups and downs. Every player and team is going to most likely have a rough start at becoming good; just remember that as you continue to play. Success comes to those who are persistent and who commit themselves to the sport of paintball, which is why you need to remain focused on getting better and not let negative thoughts discourage you.

Regularly have meetings with your teammates to help maintain their motivation for the sport of paintball. Your motivation may not be in question, yet it can be difficult to gauge the level of determination from your teammates. It is wise to consult with each individual member of your team, as well as the group as a whole to see how everyone is feeling about your progress. Address any issues that arise as soon as possible so that you can all move forward as a collective unit towards success.

Making Tough Decisions
Keep track of out how many matches you win in tournaments and against opponents in scrimmages every week. At the end of the month decide whether or not your team is progressing or if you are not making any significant improvements. In order to succeed you are going to need to make serious moves towards success, and that can call for making tough decisions.

Ask yourself if there are members of your team who are not producing enough to help your team progress. One of the toughest decisions to make while playing competitive paintball is to cut one or more members from your team. Yet if someone is not good enough to be on your team, or simply isn't practicing enough, then it is time you get rid of them. Consult with your other teammates to see how they feel and make a decision only when you are confident it is one that you won't regret.

Anyone who does not follow the strategies that are being executed should be questioned as to why they veered away from the plan. Some people simply do not understand how to follow orders, others may have seen an opportunity and tried to take advantage of a situation, and some may have just lost track of what was going on and forgot to stick to the plan. Whatever the case, speak with your team to reinforce the importance of working together and executing strategies in sync.

10

MONKEY SEE, MONKEY DO, AND OTHER WINNING METHODS

Take some time to stop playing paintball and to analyze the sport as a whole. See what other opponents and individual players are doing to increase their team's chances at winning. One strategy that is commonly overlooked in paintball is to pick up ideas from other players. There is a lot you can learn from watching others compete. You can either watch people play live or look at videos online.

What kind of weapons do other players use during matches? Do people use the same type of gun during every match, or do they change things up a bit? These are the types of questions you want to ask yourself when thinking about the mindset of other successful players. Pay close attention to the weapons the most successful paintball players use in particular matches, and if possible, inquire about why they choose a particular weapon for a specific game type.

Browse through reputable paintball forums to learn more about strategies behind using certain guns on certain fields or game types. Knowing how veterans play the game can help provide you with insight on the way they think when approaching the game. Study successful players and if you get the chance to communicate with them, pick their brains a bit to help further your knowledge of the sport.

If You Can't Beat Them, Join Them

Lose to a particular team over and over again? Consider befriending that team not to join them (although that may be an option), but to learn from them so that you can improve on your skills. Any good player knows that the tougher their competition, the better they will be in general, giving all good teams an incentive to make you and your team better. Become friends with multiple teams that are below your skill level, at your skill level, and above your skill level; take attributes that you like from each and form your own unique team strategy.

Talk to other teams if you feel yours is not living up to your potential. Committing to paintball in order to compete and win at a high level requires a certain amount of time and practice. As time goes on, you may realize that your teammates are not as committed to the sport as you are. Consult with them to determine how serious they are about competing. If they are not as committed as you are, you can join another team and still play with them for fun.

Before you commit to another team visit a few others to see who matches your play style, personality, and schedule. Once you have reached a high enough skill level, there are going to be quite a few amount of teams looking to add talent to their roster. Play some practice games with all the teams you are interested in joining, and make a decision only when you are sure you are ready to join a new team.

Study Military Strategies

Paintball strategies and tactics used in the military can be applied to your game plan in matches. In fact, flanking and a strong side attack are both tactics that were taken from the military. Look into military strategies to see which can be applied for your paintball team. Consider also speaking with someone in the military to see if they can help teach your team these types of strategies.

Apply the feint strategy to trick your opponent and work your way towards achieving victory. The feint strategy is when you draw attention to one portion of the battlefield in an attempt to distract your opponents. As they are distracted, you can focus on either grabbing

PAINTBALL STRATEGIES AND TACTICS

the objective such as the opposing team's flag, flanking the team to take them out, or taking control of a portion of the battlefield you feel is crucial towards your victory. To use the feint strategy simply have some of your teammates shoot and cause a ruckus in one area of the field and your opponents will take that as a sign that they should provide help to their teammates.

Use the refuse the flank strategy to counter your enemy's flank if you feel they are attempting this maneuver. To refuse the flank, you place the lowest amount of your teammates to defend your area and have everyone else circle your opponents. This strategy is used quite often in the military and can be seen as a counter flank maneuver.

Another military strategy that is a bit risky but that can be rewarding to apply is the human wave attack. The human wave attack is when you send out waves of your teammates out to engage the opponent in an attempt to gain more ground. This leaves your teammates extremely vulnerable for moments at a time, but it can work if executed to perfection. To execute this strategy effectively you need to provide cover fire and call out the location of every enemy you see so that you can eliminate as many opponents as possible.

TRAVELING TO GROW AS A PLAYER

Growing as a paintball player is limited when you fail to venture out to new locations to see how the game is played around the country. People from all walks of life play paintball and one of the best ways to grow as a player is to engage with a variety of players. The more you engage in combat, conversation, and naturally interact with players and teams in different parts of the country, the greater your ability to adapt as a player becomes.

Traveling for paintball does not have to cost a great deal of money, especially when you travel with your teammates. Pitching in on gas to drive a day or two in order reach a new venue for the weekend, or to compete in a tournament is fairly inexpensive. Have everyone save a bit of money for gas and hotel accommodations. Look at paintball forums to see if there are any local competitors that would not mind housing you and your teammates for a couple of days. The paintball community is a family of its own and players love to help spread the love of paintball with one another.

Before you begin traveling there is one thing you're going to want to do, and that is take note of all that goes on for you as a player and your team as you travel in paintball. From taking pictures to taking notes of your progress as a team, it's all relevant in your reasoning for venturing out around the United States to play the sport. Traveling is one of the best aspects of playing paintball, enjoy the experience every chance you get.

Start by Traveling Local

Flying out and competing in a paintball tournament is one of the most exhilarating feelings in the world. The first time you travel long distances to compete with your teammates will expose you to a different angle of paintball that you did not see before. The problem with traveling a far distance is that it is costly. Instead of using all of your money on traveling far, travel a few hours away to see how you feel about playing paintball elsewhere.

Try visiting all of your local paintball centers and then expanding from there. When you feel you are ready, plan a road trip to a paintball center a few hours away. If possible, travel when a tournament or special event is taking place so that you can compete with a variety of teams, both superior and inferior to yours. Remember, each team has some type of lesson to teach you, so take every match seriously and do your best to learn and grow as a team when you play.

When you travel for paintball, keep thorough track of your performance statistics from these away games. Look at your win-to-loss ratio when you're away from your local area to determine if you are competing to your potential. Ideally you will be getting better as time passes and your win-to-loss ratio becomes more positive. If you find that you are losing more when you travel, that could be a sign that you are either facing superior competition, or that anxiety is getting the best of your team and weakening your abilities.

Feeling anxious the first few trips you take to compete in paintball centers that you are not familiar with is normal. The best way to overcome that fear is to continue to travel and hone in on your skills as a player. As time passes, you won't feel as anxious when you travel for paintball, allowing you to show off your true skills whenever you travel to compete and play.

Save to Travel to a Major Competition or Event

Attending a major tournament or special event for paintball is part of the growing process where you learn how your team compares to others in different regions. Start saving to travel for major events if you are serious about getting better at the sport. Plan a trip once a quarter throughout the year to help give you something to look forward to while your team trains every week.

Find tournaments hosted by official paintball leagues. Leagues such as the National Speedball League, National Professional Paintball League, and the Paintball Sports Promotions are all leagues where professionals gather to compete in tournaments for money, honor, and glory. Additionally, regional leagues are hosted in all sorts of areas; visit these leagues as well so that you can expose yourself to as much of the sport as possible.

Most tournaments provide some type of cash incentive depending on your placement. Make it your team's goal to earn money as you compete in tournaments. There is no greater feeling in the world than to earn money playing something you love. Saving to travel to an event becomes much more pleasant when you can expect to earn money in the process.

Major competitions are where many people can make a real name for themselves in the sport of paintball. Winning or achieving a high level of success at a major competition can pave the road to allow you to earn passive income playing paintball, or better yet, obtaining a sponsorship to possibly make a living playing the sport. There is much to be earned by traveling as you play paintball. Consider competing in major tournaments to see how you fair against some of the best teams in the country.

12

HOW TO OBTAIN A
SPONSORSHIP FOR YOUR TEAM

Sponsorships are important for players to acquire in all types
of up and coming sports; they help players fund the costs of
paying for equipment and traveling to tournaments. Paintball sponsorships come in the form of established companies attempting to
cement themselves as the brand of choice for paintball players, or
from new companies that are interested in gaining exposure. Some
sponsorships allow you to have other sponsors; others require you to
commit to them alone.

The benefit of multiple sponsors is you can have bits and pieces
of your expenses paid for. One sponsor may be willing to pay for your
flight, another might pay for your lodging, and one might pay for all
of your equipment. This may all sound very appealing, but it can be
a burden as well. If one sponsor drops you, it can be difficult to find
another to replace them. Many potential sponsors may choose not to
sponsor you if you already have one.

Having one high-caliber sponsor gives you the added security in
knowing they are truly committed to you and will most likely help pay
for all of your expenses. Having one full sponsor, instead of relying
on multiple sources to help you afford to play paintball competitively,
definitely streamlines things. However, the downfall to having one
sponsor is that if you lose them, you are out of luck and will have to
incur all the expenses until you find another sponsor.

Promote Yourself to Attract Sponsors

New paintball players fail to recognize the important of branding oneself. Part of promotion is to get the word out about yourself to attract sponsors. The best players naturally attract sponsors to them, yet it does require some time to get your name out there until you are established.

Winning and being a player who others look up to is how you first go about attracting sponsors. Therefore, improve your individual skill to allow you to find a sponsor. Your team can attract sponsors by winning the majority of their matches as well. Both you and your team should strive for greatness if you really want to be sponsored.

Teams that are not necessarily regarded as the highest of caliber still have potential to become sponsored. Showing true dedication to the sport of paintball and providing something that gives back to the community is another way to obtain sponsorships. For instance, creating tutorial videos for how to use new paintball markers that are released, or some other type of helpful video can help get your name out in the community. Sponsors take notice of your popularity and factor that into their decision to sponsor your team.

Create physical flyers to handout to a variety of local businesses. These flyers should highlight all of the fundamental aspects of your team and reasons why it would be beneficial to sponsor you. Businesses may not react right away, yet in time they might make the decision to support you.

Posting videos of you and your team's highlights and accomplishments is a way to attract sponsors. Market both online and at local businesses you feel you have a good shot at obtaining a sponsorship. Businesses such as paintball shops that sell equipment or anything related to the sport are ideal places to start before you expand your search for a sponsor elsewhere. Essentially anywhere that wants to get their name and brand out for the paintball community to see is a potential sponsor, take that into consideration when marketing.

In your pitch to sponsors remind them that this is a mutually beneficial partnership. By aiding you to buy equipment, travel, and pay for the costs associated with playing paintball competitively, you will help market your sponsor, thus increasing their overall revenue potential on an annual basis. A sponsorship is considered an investment to grow a business, and it works. Great teams help their sponsors grow in popularity and sell more of their product or service.

Finding a sponsor to pay for all of your expenses as a team right away is very difficult. Even seasoned teams with many accomplishments can have a hard time finding a sponsor to assist with all their expenses. Consider compromising with a sponsor and receiving help to pay for at least your hotel room where you travel, or for new equipment for your team.

13

CONCLUSION

The number one rule to follow when playing paintball is to have fun when you are playing the sport. Making a team and competing in tournaments can become overwhelming for a lot of players and teams. As you all fight to earn the status as the best team it can take a lot out of you. Make sure you're having fun throughout the entire process; if you ever feel burned out from paintball take a break for a week or two and come back to the game when you feel refreshed.

There is a lot to digest as a newcomer to the sport. Everyone becomes overwhelmed with all the new terminology, rules, and in-depth thinking behind playing paintball. This game is an actual sport that requires you to be both physically and intellectually competent. The fact that you've read this book from start to finish should have provided a good foundation for your understanding of the sport so that you can apply your knowledge to a successful beginning of your career in paintball.

Reread any portion of this book about paintball that you feel you had a hard time understanding, or any area that provided information you felt was extremely valuable. Remember to relay any questions you have to veterans to provide clarity on a concept or part of paintball you simply cannot grasp. The more time you put into this sport, the better you'll be at it, so remember to be patient because you are not going to become an expert overnight.

Take pictures and videos of you and your teammates to give you all something to reflect back upon years down the line. The memories you make playing paintball can be some of the best in your life. Appreciate the sport and as your love for it grows, so should your determination and drive to win.

Bond with new players and make contacts in all of your travels. At first you may feel intimidated by approaching other paintball players, but in time you'll realize that any true professional in the sport enjoys making a new contact with someone else who genuinely has an interest in one of their passions in life as well. Join the paintball family and you will always have a network of people you can call friends.

With the massive amount of knowledge you gained from this book about paintball, the next step is to actually go out and apply everything that you've learned. Start by playing some games of paintball at a local paintball center. Newcomers are always welcomed to the sport; it is the only way it is going to grow. Respect the sport of paintball and all things associated with it and your entire experience from start to finish will be a positive influence on your life.

WEBSITES:

http://www.amazon.com/Paintball-Sports-Outdoors/
b?ie=UTF8&node=3415511

http://www.ansgear.com/

http://www.dickssportinggoods.com/category/index.
jsp?categoryId=13342723

http://www.cousinspaintball.com/

http://empirepaintball.com/

http://www.hivipaintball.com/

http://indoorextremesports.com/

http://www.islandpaintball.net/

http://paintball.com/

http://www.paintballimpact.com

http://www.sportsauthority.com/Outdoor-Equipment/Paintball-
Airsoft-Gear/category.jsp?categoryId=3084897

PAINTBALL TERMS

A

- **Arkansas Elevation** - A shooter's adjustment by aiming higher than the target's position in the sight to allow for the paintball's drop during travel rather than adjusting the sight.

B

- **Baller** – Slang for a player who participates in the sport of paintball.
- **Barrel Blocking Device (BBD)** – Barrel sock a device placed over the barrel held in place by string or elastic band . If trigger is accidently pulled it will catch unintentional rounds,
- **Bonus Ball** - A ball that is shot at an opponent after they have already been hit. (An extra shot for good measure, which is not permitted.)
- **Bounce** - A paintball making contact with a player or equipment without breaking. These paintballs 'bounce' off and do not count as an out.
- **BPS** - Balls per second. A measure of rate of fire.
- **Bunker** - An obstacle on the field of play used to block opposing players' view and field of fire.
- **B.Y.O.P** - An acronym meaning "Bring your own paint"

C

- **Cover Fire** - Supporting fire for a player who is moving out of cover.

D

- **Dry Firing** - Discharging a marker with no paintballs loaded in the hopper.

- **Double Tap** - To rapidly fire two shots at a target, increasing chances of a hit.

E

- **Eating Paint** - When a player is shot on the mouth piece of their mask.

F

- **Firing Blind** - Firing at a hidden player by using other objects for reference.(ie sounds, breath, bush movement,
- **Flank**
  - The sides and back of a player or group. The area in which they are not actively watching and aiming at.
  - A tactic to take advantage of an opponent's side by moving around them.
- **Fogged** - Term describing goggles after moisture condenses on the lens and decreases the player's visibility,

G

- **Ghost** - A player who continues to play after being shot. Usually hiding in low-activity areas to avoid being caught.

H

- **Hopper** - A container in which loose paintballs are held before falling into the breach of the marker,.
- **Hoser** - A player who shoots excessive amounts of paintballs.
- **Hot** - A bunker occupied by an opponent or a paintball marker shooting faster than the velocity limit.

I

- None.

J

- None.

K

- **Kamikaze** - A player who plays for the sole purpose of eliminating other players, with little regard to being hit.
- **Kentucky Windage** - An adjustment made by a shooter to correct for motion of the target by aiming at a point horizontal to the target's position in thesightrather than by adjusting the sight to compensate.

L

- **Leap Frog (or center peel)** -A tactic used by two or more players who alternately move and provide cover fire for each other.(oral commands sometimes given tap on back is always used.)
- **Lite it Up** - To shoot excessively or in an aggregious manner.(think Arnold)

M

- **Marker** - See paintball marker.

N

- **Newbie** - A new player

O

- **Old School** - A player or equipment that is considered to be from a previous era or "school of thought".
- **Overshoot** - To continue firing at a player after they have indicated that they are eliminated.

P

- **Paint** - Short for "paintballs".
- **Pair** - Two players designated as partners and made responsible for each other. Often, a new player and a skilled veteran will be paired to teach the new player how to play.
- **Pawn** - A player who is sacrificed to draw attention away from other players.

- **Playing On** - Situations where a player will continue to act as a live player after they are hit, or wiping a hit off.
- **Pod** - A plastic tube with a snap-closed lid that carries extra paint-balls while on the field to refill the hopper. Most hold more than 100 (generally 140) paintballs.
- **Point Blank** - At a previously agreed distance, players who catch others by surprise yell "point blank" (or something similar), to eliminate players. This minimizes bruising and bleeding from being fired upon at close range. Many recreational fields use this rule, especially when they allow young players, and it is often required in the field's insurance policy. There are numerous variations, some allowing the surprised players to choose to return fire, or requiring the surprising player to physically touch their opponent with the barrel of their marker.

Q

- None.

R

- **Ramping** - A feature that allows the marker to fire faster than the trigger is being pulled. Previously found only on cheater boards, modern electronic markers include these features and more.
- **Ref** - Short for referee.

- **Renegade** - The final player against a significant number of opposing players.
- **Roll (i.e. "roll your gun")** - Consistently firing a marker at a high rate of fire.
- **Rope** - A quickly-fired line of paintballs.
- **Run and Gun** - Running for new cover whilst providing covering fire for yourself.

S

- **Shake And Shoot** - A non-agitated gravity feed hopper. Must be occasionally bumped to prevent paintballs from jamming above the feedneck.
- **Speedball** - A variant of paintball designed for balanced, competitive play. Named after its fast games and action.
- **Spray or Splatter** - Fill of a paintball hitting an object without it actually being struck by a ball. Often does not count as an elimination.
- **Spray And Pray** - Shooting rapidly at a person without aiming.
- **Stock Class** - A style of paintball play in which markers meeting stock-class requirements are the only type of allowed. Typical stock class restrictions include manual re-cocking after every shot, limited paint capacity, and using only 12 gramcarbon dioxide cartridges.
- **Streetball** - Paintball played by those who do it simply for the love of the sport.
- **Superman** - A low, forearm dive used to move quickly underneath incoming paint.

T

- **Tank** - Containers that hold the gas that powers paintball markers. In most cases the tank is screwed directly into the marker.
- **Tape** - The side boundaries of the field.

U

- **Up** - Upgrade. Used interchangeably with mod.

V

- None.

W

- **Walking** (i.e. "walking the trigger") - Using two or more fingers to rapidly drum the trigger, resulting in a higher rate of fire than normal trigger pulling can achieve.
- **Walk On** - A player who arrives the same day as a game with no prior reservation.
- **Wipe** - Removing a hit before being called out.
- **Woodsball** - variant of paintball played in a natural setting with large boundaries. Preferred for military simulations.

X

- **X-Ball** - A variation of speedball, that has a giant X Bunker in the center of the field. X-Ball is generally a center flag game, with the flag on either the right or left side of the X bunker.

Y

- None.

Z

- **zebra** - another name for a referee